T0354585

LOVE & LIFE

Angelina Lorenzo

ISBN: 978-1-4669-6546-1 (sc)
ISBN: 978-1-4669-6547-8 (e)

Trafford rev. 10/19/2012

 www.trafford.com

North America & international
toll-free: 1 888 232 4444 (USA & Canada)
phone: 250 383 6864 ♦ fax: 812 355 4082

CONTENTS

To Juan and Esther

I Am Truly Hurt . . .

I can cover my pain with a smile,
But my eyes do not truly convince them.
The make-up for my hurt,
Yet it still remains deep.
When all I can feel is pain,
Nothing else seems to come to mind.
There is always something missing and it hurts to
know the truth, but we cannot live our lives inside
the box.
Waiting for someone to realize the hurt you hold
within.

Selfish

You only think about yourself
The plans we make are for your advantage
When we talk I have to make the first move
When I'm with you I have to lean first
It gets annoying to always be the one to
make the relationship stick
You're self-centered so you don't notice
when I'm not happy
But you're selfish
It gets me so frustrated to know that I'm the
Only one who tries to keep this relationship
running.
I'm not the glue; there should be effort on both sides.

ADDICTED

Addicted to your scent.
Addicted to your smile.
Addicted to your laugh.
And addicted to your eyes.
Everything about you just pulls me in.
But all I know is that I'm head over heels
I think I'm completely in love.

WITHOUT YOU

The sun disappears
The smile melts down
The sparks in my eyes fade away
My heart loses its fulfillment
The moon is no longer glows
I feel a emptiness; a loner
I do not have who to love
Without you neither the world nor me are the same

I Was Wrong . . .

I was so happy when we were together
My heart raced every second
My love for you was greater than my love
for cherry pie.
You were the only one on my mind
The thoughts the kept a smile on my face
I thought all this would last forever.
But I thought extremely wrong . . .

It's Hard For Me

It's hard to believe that you're telling me the truth
When you have lied, played, and hurt many
It's hard to look at you and see the boy
Who told me all those beautiful words?
It's hard to tell everyone I'm over you
When I know I'm not at all
It's hard to look at you in the eyes
& say I forgive you for all your lies.
Your eyes, your voice, you overall;
You're just a walking lie that I believed for years
My heart is a sucker, but I know what it does
People like you, I can live without
But unfortunately I decide not to . . .

Our World

It seems as if every day my life flashes before my eyes. It seems as if my life passes slow against the strain of time. It would seem as if my heart beats fast while the world goes slow. It would seem as if my head wants to explode sooner because of its ticking. It would seem as if our eyes met during this battle, as if I would die today without you. For you and me our worlds are different, but our hearts as one share the same world within us.

No Way Out

Have you ever felt like as if being yourself wasn't enough? As if you can't just be alone no matter how much you want to. As if no matter how hard you try peace never comes to you. You try to kill your stress but when you do more stress comes along & when you try to avoid it, it seems to come on stronger & stronger, draining your power to avoid things in life. When things come at you, you no longer have the power to dodge it. No matter how much you try to move, you're powerless. Your body is paralyzed in the worst position possible. Your life is frozen in your past, present, and future. But you're not frozen, your life just is. It's a never ending road of misery, joy, and tears . . . & finding your way around it is more difficult than you thought . . .

THERE ARE
THINGS . . .

There are things one's eye can't see
There are things one's eye seeks to mention
The things one's heart seems to love
The things one's heart seems to adore
There are things one's mind doesn't think of
& things one's mind doesn't know
The things we can't do or handle
The things one's life doesn't expect
& the things that we are just not ready for are the
things that make us who we are . . .

SOMETIMES I WISH . . .

Sometimes I wish I live a life of someone else.
That falling for someone was easy.
Sometimes I wish that some boys were different.
I wish they would all care like we want them to.
Sometimes I wish that love wasn't just a game.
That nothing would hurt me and that it would all
be over. Soon I wouldn't feel anything that love
throws at me, but for now I feel every pain, every
tear, and every joy and memory it brings in life.

I STAND ALONE

I live in a world where I stand alone.
Where no one can see how I truly feel.
Where no one knows what I really go through.
A place where no one understands the way I am.
Where no one can see how much my eyes truly cry.
I stand in a place where I end the day & still find a
way to smile with no one around. My smile comes
from the memories that stroll through my mind and
heart at the end of the day, knowing that it is all I
got closest to you . . .

My Life . . .

There are things in life that we deserve
The things in life that we want
There are things in that you got
The things in life that we need.
Then there are the things in life that we get, but
don't deserve & don't want
I get what I deserve & I get what's right for me
These things are not always pleasant
Most of the time they are things I didn't expect
There are things I get what I don't want, things I
get that I don't need things I get that I don't deserve
& then the things that I just simply would love, but
never seem to get . . .

PERFECTLY IMPERFECT

The perfect life that seems to go great with mine
The perfect eyes that meet mine
The perfect ears that hear my voice
The perfect hands that fit perfectly in mine
The perfect lips that touch mine
The perfect man that I could only find in dreams
The perfect relationship that seems to be only in
fairytales
The relationships in my reality are just perfectly . . .
Imperfect

No Longer Mine

Laying down on my bed
Thinking to me my life has turned
No more repeats of crying myself to sleep
My dreams have started to become sweet
My eyes are starting to see clearly
My heart is beginning to beat normal again
My life seems like it has no end
My love for you is practically over
The little love that's left is hurting me
It's what makes me depressed & frustrated
The love I had for you was deep, but I broke it
It still hurt me just not the way I expected
It kept me alive but not healthy
I was addicted to you, but found my cure
& now you are my past, present, but not my future

THE MOMENTS

The moments that sweep you off your feet
Those moments those leave you breathless and
speechless
These moments are the ones you enjoy the most
with others
Not just anyone, but your loved ones
Those are the moments you tend to love for life
even if some hurt you
You learn to live, laugh, and love
Not everyone stays loved so treasure the moments
you have with your loved ones
& never forget them no matter what

TIRED OF IT . . .

It's the life concept of love that gets me mad
You don't know what you want
& you're not always sure what you feel
My feelings for you are bipolar
One day I'm happy about you
The next day I'm not, it's very confusing
To think that the days I'm not happy about you are
the days I have reasons
All the things we been through & we're still "just
friends", but you don't talk to me
It's not good for me, so I'm letting life takes its
course
I can finally say I'm tired of it . . . & I'm tired of
you

In Love

The feeling I always get when I'm with you is
unbelievable
The feeling I get when I'm away from you is
unexplainable
The feeling I have when I'm hugging you feels
serene
The feeling I get when you talk to me I get restless
When I see, hear, or touch you I feel completely
weak & melted
I feel in love

LIFE . . .

Life should never be taken for granted
You realize what you got when it's finally gone
Your life can flash before your eyes anytime
The risk of just breathing
The bullies, street fights, love wars
They are all pointless at the end of the day
We got to learn that our desires are not there
In life you want what you don't always get
You need what you can live without
& you love what you can't have
There are many disappointments in life
We just have to learn to live with them . . .

HEARTBREAKER . . .

These feelings can't seem to go away
These feelings I experience without intending to
These feelings I adore regardless of my mood
These feelings I hate most of the day
These feelings that I know are about you
These feelings that led me right to depression
The feeling that is what it feels like
A heartbroken feeling
The one that you give every girl and don't even
care . . .

WE ARE ONE

Where am I when the one I love isn't here?
Who am I if I'm not with you?
What am I if you're not what I want you to be?
Why do I live if you're not by my side?
If I can't be with you
I might as well not be here at all
My love for you reaches the stars and the moon
We have that special bond, that special connection
We share the love no one else does
We are one . . . & without you I'm lost.

ONE GUY . . .

One guy that will prove me wrong
One guy that will care for me
One guy that will show me that he loves me
One that that will hug me when I need one
One guy that will worry about me when
something's wrong
One guy that is going to show the world that I'm
not just another girl
But I'm his girl . . . & no one can change that

WHAT DO I DO?

What do I do when the one I love is not with me?
What do you do when the one you like is acting
foolish?
What do you do when the one you gave your heart
to still has it?
What do you do when that person lost your trust?
What do you do when the one you actually trust is
not trustworthy anymore?
What to do when your worlds falls apart 7 you can't
do anything about it?
Well something you can't do is keeping these people
with you . . .

I CANNOT . . .

I cannot erase from my mind what makes me happy
I cannot forget the moments that had me speechless
I cannot leave what I love so much
I cannot just forget the harm you have done to me
& the pain you gave me after you left
I can no longer hide what I feel
The feelings just don't look like they are ever going
to go away . . .

I Will Always Love You . . .

There is a part of you I can't forget
A part of you that I need
There is a part of you that is always with me
There is just something that I will never forget
There's just something I know I will always love
The part of you that will always stay in my heart
The love & kindness that you gave me no matter
the situation
I think I could be mad at you, but I'll always love
you

THOSE PEOPLE

It's the ones who still stand by you when you're
cursing someone out for no apparent reason
Those who say sorry after you yell at them for 20
minutes about something they did
The ones that are always interested in hearing your
point of view
Those who can tell when you're hurting by taking a
glance at your eyes
The ones who make sure you always feel like one in
a million when around them
And those who always without fail pick you up,
When you're on the ground thinking there's no way
to rise above
Those are the friends worth keeping.
Those are your superheroes

By City Santiago

Printed in the United States
By Bookmasters